Bullies

Among Us

What To Do When Work's No Fun

Jean R. McFarland, Ph.D.

Published by
Fifth Dimension Strategies

Special discounts on bulk quantities of Fifth Dimension Strategies books are available
to corporations, professional associations, and other organizations. For details,
contact Fifth Dimension Strategies, Scottsdale, Arizona. Tel. 480-634-1563. Fax.
480-699-6888.

Design and layout by Mullins Creative.
www.mullinscreative.com

ISBN 978-0-9820508-0-4
Printed and bound in the United States of America

www.FifthDimensionStrategies.com
www.BadAppleSolutions.com

to Jim,
who has supported
me always

Preface

Why do I care about workplace bullies? Because I have been a target, in several different workplaces, in different industries, and of male and female bullies. I know many of you have been targets, too. Unfortunately, thirty-seven percent of employees in the United States have experienced bullying. That's approximately fifty-four million Americans.

Who should care about workplace bullies? Anyone who has been bullied. And savvy managers and employers, who know the cost to the company of sheltering bullies. Unfortunately, many employers assume the ostrich stance and bury their heads in the sand in terms of workplace bullies, or consciously choose to retain bullies, rationalizing that their "value" offsets their cost. Employers' estimates of the cost, however, frequently overlook all except the most obvious ones and don't include that of extensive collateral damage.

In general, the worse the behavior, the more disengaged is the employee and greater is the cost to the organization.

Somehow, managers perceive bullying behaviors as much less damaging than they really are, when, in fact, bullying behaviors fall on the extreme end of my Bad Apple Behavior continuum, surpassed only by physical violence.

Bad Apple behaviors cover most of the workplace behavior continuum (Fig. 1) and range from mildly uncivil behaviors to extreme bullying behaviors. Meshed with Bad Apple Behavior is Employee Disengagement. In general, the worse the behavior, the more disengaged is the employee and greater is the cost to the organization.

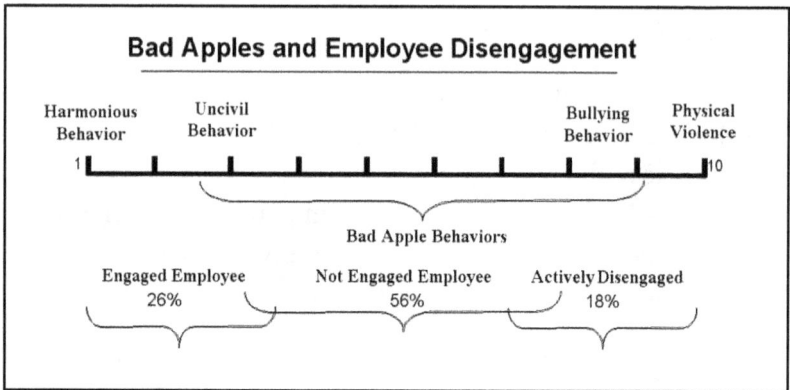

Bad Apples and Employee Disengagement

| Harmonious Behavior | Uncivil Behavior | | | | | | Bullying Behavior | Physical Violence |

Bad Apple Behaviors

Engaged Employee 26%   Not Engaged Employee 56%   Actively Disengaged 18%

Figure 1

I introduce the connection between behavior and employee disengagement as an example to show behavior cannot be isolated as a separate entity. Both positive and negative behaviors radiate outward from the center as ripples on still water and affect the entire organization, its customers and its vendors.

Jean R. McFarland, Ph.D.

Table of Contents

CHAPTER 1

Bad Apples Aren't Palatable in Any Variety

Bad Apple behaviors range from relatively mild incivilities, such as gentle teasing and cussing at whomever is handy, to extreme bullying of targeted individuals. It's important to keep in mind that bullies rarely attack physically. They practice psychological abuse, rather than physical abuse. Bullying behaviors encompass assigning unpleasant jobs or excessive workloads, exclusion, isolation, verbal abuse, sarcasm, threats, bad-mouthing, intimidation, manipulation, duplicity, authoritarianism, vindictiveness and others. Bullies endanger their targets' health and the success of their organizations.

The Doctor Was a Bully

As the only technologist for a medical researcher from England, I had the dubious honor of sharing a lab in a beautiful, new medical research facility with Dr. Knox (not his real name). He was in his late thirties, tall and lanky with naturally curly, light red hair, and bearing some resemblance to Vincent van Gogh before the ear came off.

Because I had been working with international researchers for several years, I wasn't concerned about changing to this position. In fact, I was looking forward to working with a British researcher as a new cross-cultural experience. Unfortunately, Dr. Knox wasn't looking forward to working with anyone new—but he had to. His current technologist, whom he highly favored, had been with him since he came to the United States to conduct research, but she and her husband planned to relocate soon to a different state.

Dr. Knox was a perfectionist, who rarely smiled or said anything that wasn't critical or sarcastic. Most of his communication amounted to instruction. Do this! Do that! So, when he planned to return to London for a week, I secretly rejoiced. It wasn't because I thought of skipping out of work or shirking my duties, but rather because I anticipated working without his cloudy countenance hovering over the lab.

However, Dr. Knox managed to maintain his negative influence, even in his absence. Without talking with me about projects to be worked on while he was away, he left a *LONG* list of experiments and procedures for me to complete before his return. I worked alone in that lab from 7 a.m. to 7 or 8 p.m. every day, including both weekends he was away, and managed to finish on the evening before his return.

When Dr. Knox came into the lab the next morning and I told him I had completed the work, showing him all the detailed results, he snarled, "Impossible! No one could have done all that in one week." He had *intentionally* overloaded me with work and wasn't even pleased that I had done it!

Reflecting on that and other incidents over several months, I believe his intention was to assign more than he thought I could possibly complete, so he would have "evidence" he could use to complain against me. Dr. Knox was not only a Bad Apple, he was a bully.

Research finds approximately fifty percent of men and women in workplaces are bullies. And two in every five employees experience bullying. When you think that seventy-one percent of female bullies target other women and fifty-four percent of male bullies target women, it becomes clear that the majority of targets—the recipients of the bullies' bad behavior—are women.

Research finds approximately 50% of men and women in workplaces are bullies. And two in every five employees experience bullying.

Why do these bullies behave as such? They have a psychological need for power and control, and they know they can get away with it.

Researchers Buss and Perry developed a Workplace Aggression Questionnaire that identifies many Bad Apple behaviors. Although unpleasant as any of these might be, unless they're experienced frequently, the aggressor is not a bully.

To be considered a bully, these behaviors must have been directed toward a target on a regular basis—weekly or more—for at least six months. If you're wondering how many of these behaviors it takes to make a bully, there's no designated number. However, you can be sure bullies use several of these behaviors in their personal arsenals.

Have you experienced any of these workplace aggression behaviors on a regular basis? Place a checkmark next to each you have experienced in the last six months by one or one set of individuals.

In the past six months have you regularly:

_____ 1. Been glared at in a hostile manner?

_____ 2. Been excluded from work-related social gatherings?

_____ 3. Had others storm out of the work area when you entered?

_____ 4. Had others consistently arrive late for meetings that you called?

_____ 5. Been given the "silent treatment"?

_____ 6. Not been given the praise for which you felt entitled?

_____ 7. Been treated in a rude or disrespectful manner?

_____ 8. Had others refuse your requests for assistance?

_____ 9. Had others fail to deny false rumors about you?

_____ 10. Been given little or no feedback about your performance?

_____ 11. Had others delay action on matters that were important to you?

_____ 12. Been yelled at or shouted at in a hostile manner?

_____ 13. Been subjected to negative comments about your intelligence or competence?

_____ 14. Had others consistently fail to return your telephone calls or respond to your memos or e-mail?

_____ 15. Had your contributions ignored by others?

_____ 16. Had someone interfere with your work activities?

_____ 17. Been subjected to mean pranks?

_____ 18. Been lied to?

_____ 19. Had others fail to give you information that you really needed?

_____ 20. Been denied a raise or promotion without being given a valid reason?

_____ 21. Been subjected to derogatory name-calling?

_____ 22. Been the target of rumors or gossip?

_____ 23. Shown little empathy or sympathy when you were having a tough time?

_____ 24. Had co-workers fail to defend your plans or ideas to others?

_____ 25. Been given unreasonable workloads or deadlines — more than others?

_____ 26. Had others destroy or needlessly take resources that you needed to do your job?

_____ 27. Been accused of deliberately making an error?

_____ 28. Been subjected to temper tantrums when disagreeing with someone?

_____ 29. Been prevented from expressing yourself (for example, interrupted when speaking)?

_____ 30. Had attempts made to turn other employees against you?

_____ 31. Had someone flaunt his or her status or treat you in a condescending manner?

_____ 32. Had someone else take credit for your
work or ideas?

_____ 33. Been reprimanded or "put down" in front of others?

(Questions adapted from works of Buss and Perry.)

Who are your Bad Apples?

1. _____

2. _____

3. _____

Before you go further with this exercise, think about someone
at work whom you feel good about—someone who supports
you and appreciates your work, a Good Apple. In Figure 2, on
a scale of 1 – 10, where 1 is a Grade-A beautiful apple and 10 is
a totally rotten apple, where would you place your supportive
Good Apple and where would you hang the Bad Apples? Base
this on how you feel about their behavior toward you, and your
responses to the aggressive-behaviors questions.

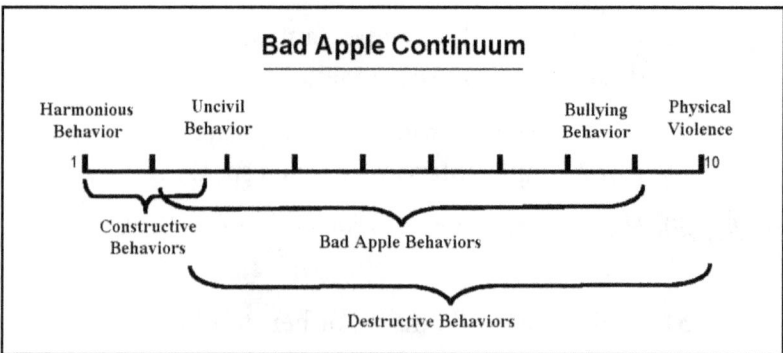

Figure 2

CHAPTER 2

Not All Bad Apples Are at the Bottom of the Barrel

Eighty-one percent of bullies are bosses, with the power to terminate their targets' employment. These bullies have a compulsive need to control others, but lack control in their own lives. They have low self-esteem and consider their targets' capabilities a threat. They aim to drive their targets out, and in eighty-two percent of cases, the bullies win, as their targets quit their jobs to escape.

The idea that bullies target weak or vulnerable individuals is a myth. Generally, their insecurity leads them to target people they perceive as superior to them in some way—better educated, advancing quicker, more attractive, more competent, more talented, better liked, whatever. Their perceptions may be totally inaccurate but, nevertheless, the target is seen as a threat that must be dealt with.

> *Bullies target whomever they perceive as superior (threatening) to them in some way.*

The Killer Bee

The head of a department in a very large university was bullying a part-time employee, who was also a graduate student in the department. Sharon was a very attractive, blond-haired woman in her late thirties, working on a Master's degree. The department head was a very attractive, black-haired woman, also in her late thirties. She was quite outspoken and often remarked she had converted from Catholicism to Judaism just to spite her mother. She also seemed compelled to frequently report on her alternative lifestyle and how deeply that offended her mother.

Typical of some bullies, the department head made disparaging comments about Sharon's work performance, in the presence of Sharon and other members of the department. Also typical of many bullies, she chose to make direct attacks when she thought no one would see or hear.

Late one dark, rainy afternoon when classes were over and most offices were empty, I was walking down a dimly lighted hallway on the top floor of one of the older, brick university buildings, headed toward the office where I worked part-time while pursuing a graduate degree.

As I passed one of the offices set aside for student employees, I inadvertently witnessed the department head intently leaning across Sharon's desk, holding a can of insect spray clearly labeled in big black letters: "For Killing Wasps." She was holding the can pointed directly at Sharon's face—with her finger on the button, and snarling, "This is what we do to a wasp, W-A-S-P." The reference, of course, was to White Anglo-Saxon Protestants. Interestingly, the department head was white and Anglo-Saxon, but not Protestant.

Workplace bullies don't suddenly become bullies when they enter the workforce. More than likely, they were playground bullies, dealing with the same insecurities as children that they harbor as adults. Even worse, they now deal with those insecurities in the same way as they did on the playground: attempting to browbeat and undermine the self-confidence and reputation of their targets.

Looking again at the Bad Apple Continuum (Fig. 3), we're reminded that not all Bad Apples are bullies. There may be many other reasons for Bad Apple behaviors. Chronic diseases such as diabetes, in which blood glucose fluctuations can cause mood swings and behavioral changes, are one example.

Low levels of emotional intelligence are another example and bring to mind celebrities who throw chairs and pitch phones at their employees when they're upset. Another is chronic stress due to downsizing and the increased workloads that go with cutting back on employees, but not on expectations.

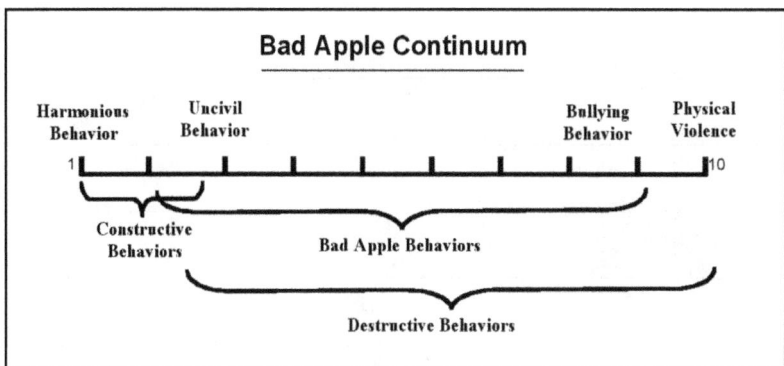

Bad Apple Continuum

| Harmonious Behavior | Uncivil Behavior | | Bullying Behavior | Physical Violence |

Constructive Behaviors

Bad Apple Behaviors

Destructive Behaviors

Figure 3

Under-qualification for one's job, whether on the line or higher up the ladder, causes stress and insecurity that can erupt in conflict with other employees.

Additional reasons abound, but the good news is that many lesser behaviors can be remedied if the Bad Apple is willing to try. Bullies, however, are less likely to want to change. Why? Because bullies receive greater rewards from their negative behaviors than they would from reforming, at least in their own minds.

If you're a target, why do you think the bully has chosen you? Record your thoughts below.

_____

_____

_____

_____

_____

_____

_____

_____

_____

_____

CHAPTER 3

Bullies:
From Screamers to
Scoundrels

The majority of bullying behaviors in the workplace fall into one or more of these four categories: Snarly Screamers, Chronic Critics, Gatekeepers, and Two-faced Scoundrels.

1. **The Snarly Screamer** rants and raves and screams at the target for any reason—or no reason. One of my colleagues found a Snarly Screamer in her client company. Ms. Snarly Screamer controlled everything and everyone within her realm, to the point that her team members

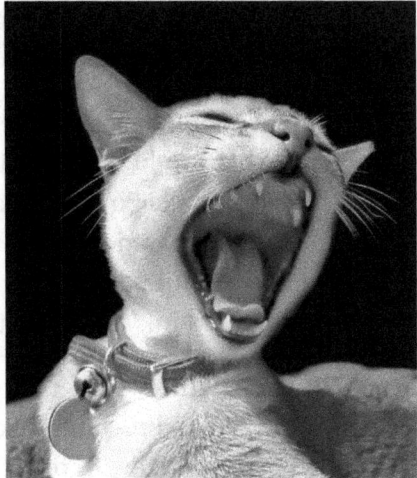

feared to comment or offer suggestions in meetings without looking toward her first for her consent.

2. **The Chronic Critic**. You can't do anything right for Chronic Critics. They watch for your mistakes, and if they don't see any, they create "errors." They are overly critical of everything their targets say and do.

The Chronically Critical Professor
One of my bullies was on my master's degree thesis committee. This female professor fancied herself a perfectionist. She was also a controlling critic, but I didn't understand that at the time. I believed it would be more difficult to gain her approval of my thesis document, but I also thought that would make my thesis stronger and better. Although as skilled in grammar and writing as the professor, I prepared my manuscript with great attention to detail and submitted it for her approval. It came back, showing in red ink *her* great attention to detail!

I disagreed with several of her edits, but I made the changes she indicated and re-submitted the manuscript. Again, it came back covered with red edits and little red smiley faces she had added—to cushion the criticisms, I guess. (I've disliked little hand-drawn smiley faces ever since! ☺)

Again, I made the changes and got the same results. Two things were becoming obvious: first, there was no way to satisfy her; and, second, most of the last edits she required reverted the writing to what I had *originally* submitted. Unbelievable!

At that point, I lost all professional respect for that professor. She continued to bully me in other ways until I graduated from the program without her approval.

3. **Gatekeepers** use various means of sabotage including withholding or detouring materials, so what you need to do your job is incomplete or delayed, and you get blamed for not meeting the deadlines!

Opportunity Flies Out the Window
The C-Level executive of a humongous global manufacturing company had just seen an ad on TV that caught his attention as no others had—not for the product advertised, but for the quality of the production. "Find the producer of that ad," he told his staff. They did.

Theresa was escorted first into the executive's exquisite antechambers, offered refreshments served in hand-cut crystal, and left alone. Soon Mr. Borbon (not his real name) entered the room and escorted Theresa into his luxurious top-floor office, walled with windows featuring aerial views of the city and rivers below.

Beyond the beautiful setting, Theresa was impressed with Mr. Borbon's genuineness, intense professionalism, and intellect, yet lack of pretension. He asked about the TV ad she had produced: "How long did it take?"

Her answer: "Two weeks." Mr. Borbon was astounded. He exclaimed that he couldn't get an ad produced internally in less than six months.

They talked about ideas for his advertising and, before she left, Theresa's company was contracted. His immediate staff arranged for her to meet the internal people who would be her contacts. That's when the trouble started.

Most of the team Theresa would work with wanted to cooperate, but it soon became apparent they were exceedingly stressed due to one bully on board, a Gatekeeper. Jerome withheld information from his team and from Theresa. He lied about receiving information from both higher and lower levels. He did everything he could to stall the project to protect his turf, and to make it look as if Theresa had lied about the short time factor for production. Although other team members were familiar with Jerome's Bad Apple behavior, they also feared him and would not or could not speak out against him.

As in 82% of bullying cases, the bully stayed on board, and the target left.

In addition to being a Gatekeeper, Jerome was a Two-faced Scoundrel, at least initially. He was pleasant enough to

Theresa's face but, behind her back, he bad-mouthed her work and blamed her for the production delay.

Ultimately, Theresa fired the company as her client. What began as an exciting venture with long-term potential ended in stress and loss of time and money that Theresa had invested in the project. As in eighty-two percent of bullying cases, the bully stayed on board, and the target left.

4. **The Two-Faced Scoundrel** is nice to your face, but then attacks behind your back.

The worse the Bad Apples, the more they interfere with other employees' work and are hazardous to employee and organizational health.

Bullying is
"a systematic campaign of
interpersonal destruction
that has no reasonable
place in the modern
workplace, but is accepted."

~ Gary Namie, Ph.D.,
Workplace Bullying Institute

CHAPTER 4

How Do Bullies Sicken Their Targets?

W hen I ask my audiences who among them has been bullied, many hands go up. If the audience is all women, the response is well over fifty percent. Some women tell me they didn't know they were being bullied. They thought they just had really mean bosses. Some women tell me they think *they* have been bullies.

Remember the 1988 movie, *Working Girl*, starring Sigourney Weaver and Melanie Griffith? And the more recent movie, *The Devil Wears Prada*, starring Meryl Streep? Then there's the TV show, *Ugly Betty*. These are supposed to be humorous entertainment, but if you view them from the perspective of bullying, they aren't so funny. The "humor" is always at someone else's expense.

Unfortunately, the targets of bullies hesitate to report what's happening. They feel it's their problem, or that no one will believe them, or they're ashamed. Often, targets think they're alone—they have no one to go to. As a result, forty percent of targets never file a complaint. Only three percent file lawsuits.

In many cases, when targets do seek help, it's easier for everyone to downplay or ignore it.

In many cases, if targets do seek help, there's no procedure or desire to deal with it, so it's easier for everyone else to downplay or ignore it, as in the following case of the conservationist.

Conserving Nature, But Not Employees

After a year of feeling intimidated, humiliated and abused by her male boss, and having her career destroyed by his defamation and undermining of her work, a respected and seasoned female conservationist went out on the Carrizo Plain of California, shot her two beloved dogs, covered their bodies with a blanket, and shot herself.

She left a detailed journal of everything she had been through, and all the reports she had submitted about her boss's behavior toward her. She had gone through all the appropriate channels to seek help, but her reports were ignored: Her boss had support from higher up the bureaucratic ladder. Fortunately, because of her journal, there was an investigation after her death. Of course, that was too late for her.

Figure 4 shows how bullying behaviors affect targets. The already stressed targets suffer loss of self-esteem and self-confidence. They also may suffer psychological and physical illness. Consequently, motivation to perform well at work deteriorates. In some cases, as with the conservationist, the target's reputation is so damaged by the bully that she cannot remain in her chosen profession.

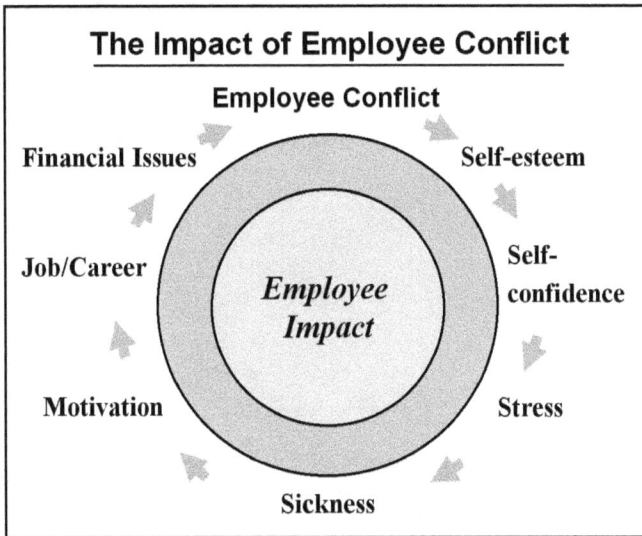

The Impact of Employee Conflict

Employee Conflict

Financial Issues

Self-esteem

Job/Career

Employee Impact

Self-confidence

Motivation

Stress

Sickness

Figure 4

The Steel Headband

Most cases of bullying don't end as tragically as that of the conservationist. In one case when I was a target, the stress from continuous bullying behavior caused me to have terrible headaches. It reminded me of when I was a child, there was a TV ad for a pain reliever that depicted a woman with an inch-wide steel band around her forehead which seemingly grew tighter and tighter as her pain became excruciating. I knew, of course, that couldn't be possible—it was just an ad—until I experienced the tightening of that one-inch steel band around my forehead.

For six months, I tolerated the bullying behaviors and the daily headaches—all the time wondering WHY? Why was I disliked so much? I wasn't used to this treatment, and no matter how hard I tried, I couldn't seem to change it. I didn't want to quit, because I'm not a quitter. To quit meant to fail. Eventually, stress and common sense prevailed, and I did leave that job. Fortunately, I *could* leave. Some targets feel they can't leave, and don't, until their health is so compromised, they can't function.

"When fear rears its ugly head, people focus on protecting themselves, not on helping their organizations improve."

~ W. Edwards Deming

CHAPTER 5

How to Deal with Bad Apple Poisoning

In all the workplaces where I experienced, witnessed, or consulted on bullying behaviors, there was essentially no laughter, but plenty of the monster called stress. There was never the kind of humor I call jocularity. That's a funny word, meaning full-of-fun, playful, non-threatening humor.

Believe it or not, jocularity is actually measurable. The University of Southern California has tested subjects both before and after laugh sessions, and found that laughing lowers blood pressure, releases natural painkillers (endorphins), and boosts the immune system. At the moment we experience humor, feelings of depression, anger, and anxiety dissolve. Employees relax and are more productive. They become more engaged in their work.

Laughter not only increases camaraderie, but also is great for team building—two factors that make it more difficult for bullies to psychologically and physically isolate targets. Some organizations, such as General Electric, IBM, 3M, Lockheed, the IRS, and The International Embalmers Association, are tuning in to jocularity and actively encouraging humor in the workplace. Now, you know if humor works for an embalmers' association, it must be good!

In the movie, *"The Bucket List,"* starring Jack Nicholson and Morgan Freeman, one item on Freeman's list of things he wants to do before he dies is to laugh until he cries, and he finally does—on his deathbed!

For goodness sakes, don't wait that long! Laugh at work. Laugh at your bully, if you can do so without repercussions. It helps if you can think of something besides the bully's behavior toward you when he or she is ranting. Look directly at her and ask yourself, "I wonder what she'd look like if she were bald." Or what if he had Brussels sprouts sticking out of his ears? This allows you to maintain eye contact, but envision and think outside the ranting.

In cases of bullying, Human Resources, managers, and the organization all have responsibility in dealing with bullies but, without company policies in place, they probably won't do anything. The target must take defensive action. As Eleanor Roosevelt said, "No one can make you feel inferior without your consent."

Antidotes to Bad Apple Poisoning

1. **Speak Up!** Bring it out in the open. If you're a target, you're probably not the only one, and you can be almost certain other people know something is going on, but aren't saying anything. Tell your family, friends, co-workers, and manager (unless the manager is your bully or supports your bully). Build a supportive network. Don't keep the

situation to yourself or you'll surely self-destruct. Sharing your concern greatly lightens the load by externalizing the problem.

2. **Decide to Confront or Not.** Consider talking directly to your Bad Apple. This approach can work successfully on the milder (left) side of the behavior continuum, but is unlikely to work with extreme bullies. In fact, confronting bullies usually worsens the situation.

Bad Apple Without Cause

Several years ago, I was a Bad Apple and didn't know it. I saw Mary almost every workday, and we always talked for a few minutes. She was intelligent, witty, and had a great personality and sense of humor. She was one of those people who attracts others and generates goodwill by just being there. In short, Mary sparkled.

I always enjoyed her company and good nature and thought of her as very laid back and easy to talk and joke with. But I failed to see Mary's deep sensitivity under the sparkle, until one day when she asked me not to tease her anymore. I was dumbfounded! I hadn't realized I'd been teasing her or that my words were hurtful.

Of course, after Mary's request, I more carefully screened my dialogue with her to avoid further interpretations of teasing. Although, in my eyes, Mary still sparkled, our conversations lost spontaneity as I cautiously monitored my words.

The lesson I learned was that we can never be sure of how people really feel under their public persona, so we must be sensitive to others' sensibilities and how we impact people. Lack of awareness could make us Bad Apples without cause.

23

3. **Record.** Keep a record or journal of each incident, including the time, place, and people present or nearby who may have heard the exchange (Fig. 5). Record words spoken and your actual observations, such as "the veins on the side of his neck bulged and pulsated." Do *not* use emotion-laden accounts. They don't stand up as accurate details. If it becomes necessary to use your records in court or mediation, emotional accounts are more likely to work against you than for you.

4. **Report** to Human Resources.Use your detailed record that presents just the facts, but be aware that reporting doesn't guarantee action. In sixty-two percent of reported bullying cases, the situation is made worse or ignored.

5. **Educate** yourself and others about bullies, bullying, and self-preservation. Do you have recourse within the company, based on laws and internal policies? Does your organization have an Employee/Workplace Bill of Rights? Become familiar with the Healthy Workplace Bill, authored by David Yamada, J.D. and Gary Namie, Ph.D. In part, Yamada and Namie's Healthy Workplace Bill reads,

> "This bill would make it an unlawful employment practice to subject an employee to an abusive work environment, as defined, and would specify that an employer is vicariously liable for a violation committed by its employee, but would prescribe certain affirmative defenses. The bill would also make it an unlawful employment practice to retaliate against an employee, because the employee has opposed an unlawful employment practice under the bill or has made a charge, testified, assisted, or participated in an investigation or proceeding under the bill."

Bad Apple Antidotes

1. Speak Up!
2. Decide to Confront or Not
3. Keep Records
4. Report Bully's Behavior
5. Educate Yourself
6. Promote Anti-bullying Policies
7. Build a Case
8. Protect Your Health

Variations of this bill have been introduced in several states. Targets should learn whether it has been introduced in the state of their employment and its current status.

Snarly by Design

In a small business setting of only 20 people, including the owner, a male Snarly Screamer targeted a talented, young female designer. Targeted means he chose her as his verbal punching bag and "beat" on her daily. Consequently, Charlotte developed the classic symptoms of a target under stress. She feared going to work every morning. Just thinking about it made her heart pound and her chest tighten until she could hardly breathe. She began taking sick days for medical appointments and sometimes just to avoid having to see Mr. Snarly.

Realizing only she could do anything about her situation, Charlotte attended several classes on developing assertiveness and self-confidence. Although she still tightened up at the thought of going to work in the morning, she finally gathered the nerve to tell him after his next tirade that she didn't like the way he treated her. At that moment, the female owner walked in, heard the young woman's words, and told Charlotte she had to apologize to Mr. Snarly. Stress and reaction to the unjust verdict caused Charlotte to flee the room in tears, but the owner didn't relent. Charlotte was forced to apologize.

Gather data on how your bully's behavior affects the company's bottom line: turnover, absenteeism, and loss of a customer or preferred vendor, for example.

Shortly after this incident, Mr. Snarly resigned for unrelated reasons. A few months later, Charlotte was accepted into a university graduate program and walked out of that company without looking back.

6. **Promote** policies and procedures in your company for reporting and handling Bad Apples. If your organization doesn't have a system in place, start an active campaign.

7. **Build a Case.** Gather data on how your bully's behavior affects the company's bottom line: turnover rates, absenteeism, and loss of a customer or preferred vendor, for example. Make a detailed, cost-based argument to your superiors, if you can do so without fearing reprisals.

8. **Protect** your health. Take time off if your health is jeopardized. If you think you're headed for panic attacks or depression, see a doctor. Don't allow yourself to go down that slippery slope. No job is worth your health.

Remember, moving on is not giving up. You may have to leave rather than suffer long-term physical and psychological damage. But submit a record of the bullying you've endured

Moving on is not giving up.

and a report of the cost to the company to both your superiors and to Human Resources before you leave. Make it part of your exit interview and request that a copy go in your file. Also, request a copy of your file. Then talk to your legislators if you favor making bullying illegal.

So far, unlike sexual harassment and discrimination, workplace bullying is not illegal. Several states—California, Connecticut, Hawaii, Kansas, Massachusetts, Missouri, Montana, New Jersey, New York, Oklahoma, Oregon, Vermont, and Washington— have started legislation by introducing versions of the Healthy Workplace Bill. To date, however, no bills have passed into law despite repeated attempts.

Is your workplace fun?

Have aggressive behaviors interfered with your work? How?

_____

_____

_____

_____

What behaviors have had a negative emotional impact on you?

_____

_____

_____

Figure 5 represents a log page you can create to record and describe bullying incidents. Be sure to include the name of the perpetrator in your log.

Date & Place	Witness	Incident	Words Spoken	Physical Observations	Outcome
05.29.08, 1:35pm My cubicle	Jane Doe	Banged his hand loudly on desk behind me, startling me and causing me to jump.	"Just wanted to see if you were awake."	Sneer on face	He left. My heart pounded.
05.30.08, 10:30am Coffee room	John Smith Jane Doe	Came into coffee room and shouted at me in front of other employees.	"Why the hell aren't you at your desk? Your report isn't in yet."	Mr. Snarly was red-faced. Veins at temples and sides of neck were bulging and pulsating.	My heart was pounding. I was shaking. Skipped break. Went back to my desk.

Figure 5 (Names in log are fictitious.)

CHAPTER 6

It's Easier to Hire Smart than to Fire Bullies

Some Bad Apples can change their behaviors if they want to change, but consider where they hang on the Bad Apple Continuum (Fig. 6). As behavior progressively worsens along the continuum, moving from Uncivil Behavior to Bullying Behavior, change becomes increasingly more difficult and less likely. Long-time bullies aren't likely to change. Remember, they've probably been bullies since childhood and have been rewarded for or by their bullying behaviors. It's a way of life.

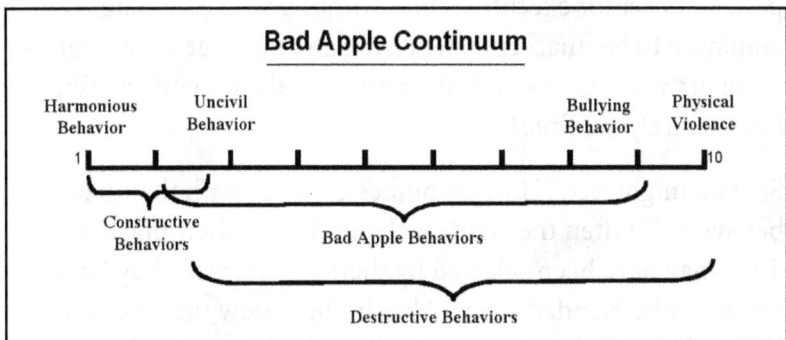

Bad Apple Continuum

| Harmonious Behavior | Uncivil Behavior | | | | | | Bullying Behavior | Physical Violence |

1 ——————————————————— 10

Constructive Behaviors

Bad Apple Behaviors

Destructive Behaviors

Figure 6

However, if Bad Apple behaviors, including bullying, are brought to the perpetrators' attention, they should be given opportunities to improve. **Anger Management** training is most commonly offered. Within or in addition to anger management training should be training to improve communication and emotional intelligence skills.

Workplace bullies often have been bullies since childhood.

It's a way of life.

Communication skills certainly should include interpersonal communication skills, under which come cussing and swearing. Did you know there's a Cuss Control Academy? There is, and it's based in Illinois. Isn't it interesting that in sixty-two percent of cases, when employers are made aware of bullying, they either make the situation worse or ignore it, but thirty-six percent of bosses surveyed in the United States have issued formal warnings about cussing? In fact, according to a survey conducted by the Cuss Control Academy, cussing topped the list of *most punishable* offenses.

In a survey of senior executives by TheLadders.com, an online provider of senior talent in the six-figure range, eighty-one percent of senior executives find working with a cussing employee to be unacceptable. Firing an employee for bad office manners was cited by seventy percent of the executives. Yet, bullies rarely are fired!

So, you might ask, "How do bullies get away with their bad behaviors?" Often they endear themselves to their managers. They may have been selected by their superiors or they have somehow befriended them. Also, bullies know the rules and follow them when other people are present. Most of their bullying is on the sly. It works much like child abuse and spousal abuse, wherein the bruises are inflicted when and where they won't be noticed.

They've mastered their techniques and can antagonize targets without penalty, because no law is being broken. They presume no one else can see what's happening, and from experience, they know Human Resources and management look the other way.

"How do bullies get away with their bad behaviors?"

Often they endear themselves to their managers.

Part of understanding and responding appropriately to others is what we call Emotional Intelligence. Emotional Intelligence involves knowing our hot buttons. What causes knee-jerk reactions? How can we control our reactions, so we can manage our responses?

Emotional Intelligence is competence in self-knowledge, self-control, and managing relationships. Competence in these three important areas—self-knowledge, self-control, and managing relationships—is not only valuable for self-development and improving personal effectiveness, but it's also valuable to employees' departments or teams and their organizations.

Employees should be recruited and selected based on what are wrongly called "soft" skills, as well as their technical knowledge and skills. Skills and attributes so critically important for success deserve more attention and a more positive label than "soft." They have always been the *real* hard skills.

Soft skills have always been the REAL hard skills.

"Bullies see the world with a paranoid's eye. They feel justified in retaliating for what are actually imaginary harms."

~ Kenneth Dodge,
Psychologist,
Vanderbilt University

CHAPTER 7

Law of Constraints: Squeezing Good Apples Can Bruise Them

Assessments of an applicant's personality, emotional intelligence, social style, and managerial style reveal much more about how the applicant will "fit" in the organization than a review of education and technical skills can show.

Other factors include appropriateness of employees for their position. If promoting an employee from, let's say, technical analyst to manager of a technical unit, will the employee be qualified for and comfortable in the managerial position? Or will frustration from having to deal with people issues rather than technical issues lead to undue stress and then to Bad Apple behaviors? In other words, will the employee "fit?"

Think of it as a marriage. Would or did you choose a spouse because of technical prowess in the kitchen, or ability to create databases? I hope not. Probably, your choice included "fit" of personalities, interests, motivation, intelligence, and many other factors. The same "fit" is necessary when selecting employees, in order to maintain a positive environment, encourage employee engagement, increase productivity, and improve retention. The better the fit, the greater the motivation and sense of belonging, so the fewer constraints on productivity.

Candidates Most Likely to Become Highly Engaged Employees Are …

- *Flexible*
- *Emotionally mature*
- *Passionate about their work*
- *Self-motivated and have high standards*
- *Positive*
- *Able to laugh at themselves*

Loosely translated, the Law of Constraints states the speed of any process can be only the speed of the slowest, most constrained members in the process. We can have exceptionally intelligent and creative employees, but if they aren't selected and prepared for the particular situation, they slow down everyone and become liabilities rather than assets. In other words, inputs and outputs are not the key; the bottleneck or "fit" is the key.

The better the fit, the greater the motivation and sense of belonging, so the fewer constraints on productivity.

Due to constraints, only forty-four percent of projects finish on time. They usually take more than twice as long as originally planned, and costs are nearly double the amount projected.

It's like trying to make applesauce by squeezing the whole beautiful apple into the bottle. It's slow, inefficient, and the final product might be contaminated. But when the apples are carefully selected and prepared for synergistic compatibility with the other constituents, they fit, and produce much sweeter applesauce.

If conflict of all types—from petty misunderstandings to major employee conflict—was reduced, imagine how performance, productivity, and the bottom line could improve!

"Organizations just hemorrhage resources when they allow [bullying] to continue."

~ Pamela Lutgen-Sandvik, Assistant Professor, Communication & Journalism, UNM

CHAPTER 8

Bad Apple Poisoning Crosses Cultural Boundaries

Although Bad Apples aren't palatable in any variety, sometimes they don't know they're behaving badly. Remember, our behaviors are shaped by the cultures we grow up in. An acceptable behavior in one culture might be unacceptable in another—as in the following case.

Misunderstanding Culture-Based Behaviors Leads to High Costs

A Japanese manufacturer invited me to its North American headquarters to address some cross-cultural problems. Typically, all executives and administrators were Japanese males, and in this case, ninety-nine percent of all employees were Americans. The rest were Canadians.

Day after day, whenever one of the Japanese executives, Mr. Yashimoto (not his real name), summoned his female American assistant to his office, he almost immediately began ranting and raving at her for what she perceived as no reason whatsoever.

He never explained to her that he was highly insulted and angry because every time he called her into his office, she sat down and crossed her legs—one knee over the other. Women across the United States and Europe often sit that way, and she had no idea that, from his cultural perspective, only a prostitute would sit with crossed legs in the presence of a man.

As you would expect, the tension mounted every day and the assistant began having migraine headaches and other physical symptoms. She had to take numerous sick days for medical appointments and illness. When she was at work, her performance was way below par, due to her stress level and consequent physical problems.

Finally, she had to take a medical leave of absence and eventually resigned from the company. She continued to suffer physical and psychological problems stemming from the stress of that situation, and ultimately filed a lawsuit against the company.

Let's take a closer look at this case, because a lot is going on here. The problem started with a misunderstanding about a behavior so common to Western women that it isn't even thought about by women *or* men, but it ended in a lawsuit of hundreds of thousands of dollars. What happened to the target in between?

1. **Stress** continued to build for both the executive and the assistant, but primarily for the assistant, due to the daily verbal attacks.

2. **Illness.** The target (assistant) experienced both psychological and physical medical symptoms.

3. **Absenteeism.** The assistant missed many days of work, due not only to illness, but also to fear of having to face her boss and his verbal beatings.

4. **Presenteeism.** When the assistant was at work, she so dreaded another attack by her boss that she couldn't focus on her work. She was present in body, but not in mind.

5. **Performance and Productivity** declined because of the assistant's illnesses, absenteeism, and presenteeism. See how the effects of stress continue to pile up, one on top of another, until there's either a crash or an explosion?

What were some of the consequences for the company?

1. **Increased Cost.** Paid medical leave; increased employee insurance rates; salary for non-productive time; cost of recruiting, selecting, and training a replacement assistant; and lawsuits.

2. **Productivity Affected.** There's an old saying that goes something like this: A chain is only as strong as its weakest link. In other words, the Law of Constraints was active. When productivity of one employee declines, the ripple effect is felt throughout the unit or organization.

3. **Reputation Tarnished.** Employees' comments and stories outside their workplace impact their organization's reputation. Their comments not only influence decisions of people contemplating seeking employment in the organization, but also influence consumers' decisions to purchase the company's products.

4. **Bad Press.** When large organizations are sued for any form of employee harassment, it hits the papers. Invariably, when

one suit is filed, a rash of suits occurs, which held true in this case, as well.

Was Mr. Yashimoto a Bad Apple? Yes, definitely, from an American behavior standpoint.

Did he know he was behaving badly by American standards? Originally, he didn't.

Why? Because this was a cross-cultural incident in which neither the Japanese nor the Americans had been educated in cross-cultural communication and management. They didn't understand each other's traditions; neither were they aware of significant differences in their managerial styles, acceptable workplace behaviors, and acceptable behavior toward female employees. Although the incident blew out of proportion and erupted due to cross-cultural incompetence, the results were as devastating as if the bully intentionally tried to drive out his target.

Here's why the Japanese-American case resembled bullying:

- It took place over an extended period of time. By definition, negative behaviors are bullying when they take place against a target repeatedly for at least six months.

- It was abusive treatment that included browbeating language and/or behavior.

- It was unwelcome, destructive, and persistent behavior that interfered with the assistant's performance of her job.

- It caused psychological and/or physical illness.

- Eventually, the target left the company due to illness.

This is a case of cross-cultural bullying without intent, so I would hang Mr. Yashimoto about here on the Bad Apple continuum (Fig. 7):

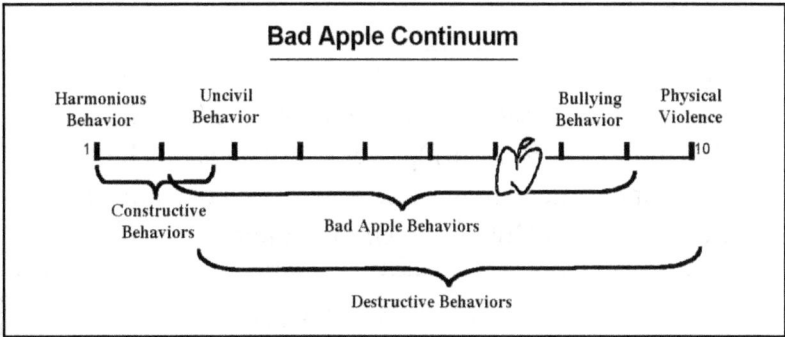

Figure 7

Had both the Japanese and the Americans been culturally prepared to work together, this could have been avoided. The cost of counseling and training would have been minimal, compared to the costs of a poisoned work environment, decline in performance, absenteeism, high staff turnover, and lawsuits.

Furthermore, the costs of recruiting, selecting, and training a new assistant might be wasted if she suffers the same consequences as the first assistant. Without cross-cultural preparation or intervention, this scenario is bound to simply rewind and play again every time a new assistant is brought on board for this administrator.

When men perceive men and women's roles as clearly distinct in society, they are likely to dominate women, and their motivators are traditionally *Masculine* values, such as assertiveness, achievement, competition, and a need to succeed. Traditionally, these cultures are termed *Masculine* cultures.

But when men and women's roles are perceived to overlap, relationship-building, service, care for the weak, nurturance, and solidarity prevail. These cultures traditionally are termed *Feminine* cultures, because they exhibit traditionally *Feminine* values. The degree to which cultures are Masculine or Feminine varies from culture to culture.

In Figure 8, you can see that although both the U.S. and Japan are Masculine cultures, scoring over 50, Japan is much more so. In fact, it has the highest masculinity score of all the nations researched in Geert Hofstede's seminal study.

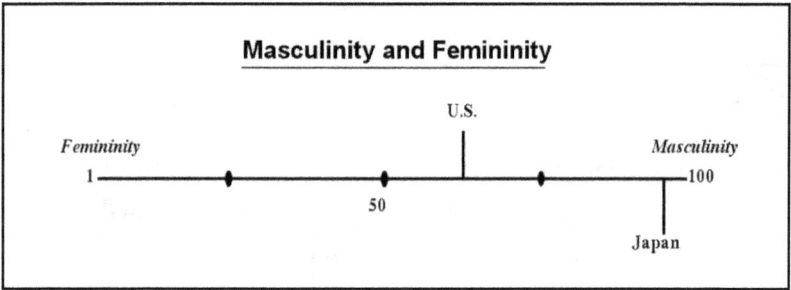

Masculinity and Femininity

Femininity

U.S.

Masculinity

1 ──────────●──────────●──────────│──────────●──────────────100

50

Japan

Figure 8

With Japan's high Masculinity score, it would be logical to expect that males would dominate females, even females of another culture. However, when people become aware of the other side's cultural expectations and respect the consequences of violating those expectations, they can learn to manage their knee-jerk reactions. In fact, with training and practice, they are likely to understand the source and meaning of culture-based behaviors and won't have jerky knees!

Here are some of the main contributors to this cross-cultural case:

- Misunderstood, culture-based behaviors

- Interpersonal (social) communication styles differed

- Low level of emotional intelligence

- Conflict between U.S. and Japanese managerial styles

- Cross-cultural incompetence of both parties

Unfortunately, this incident was never addressed. It was allowed to progress until the target's health seriously declined—both psychologically and physically.

Figure 9 depicts the critical chain of events that often occurs in the workplace when cultures cross. But it also shows the positive path to cross-cultural competence that occurs when training defuses emotions and turns the corner, away from conflict.

1. The spark that sets off the escalation of emotions is generally due to misunderstanding the behaviors of people from a different culture and, therefore, not respecting the differences.

   Our brains respond with emotion 80,000 times quicker than with logic.

2. We not only misinterpret the behaviors but we take them as personal affronts.

3. That can lead to negative emotions that get blown completely out of proportion and flash into conflict. Productivity plummets during this disruption.

4. Through interventions such as cross-cultural competence training, participants learn and come to understand how and why cultural behaviors developed and what they mean. This helps to dissipate the flash-point anger to a reasonable, less emotional level.

At this point, if participants are flexible and emotionally mature, we begin to see positive changes in behavior that with continued practice lead to cross-cultural competence.

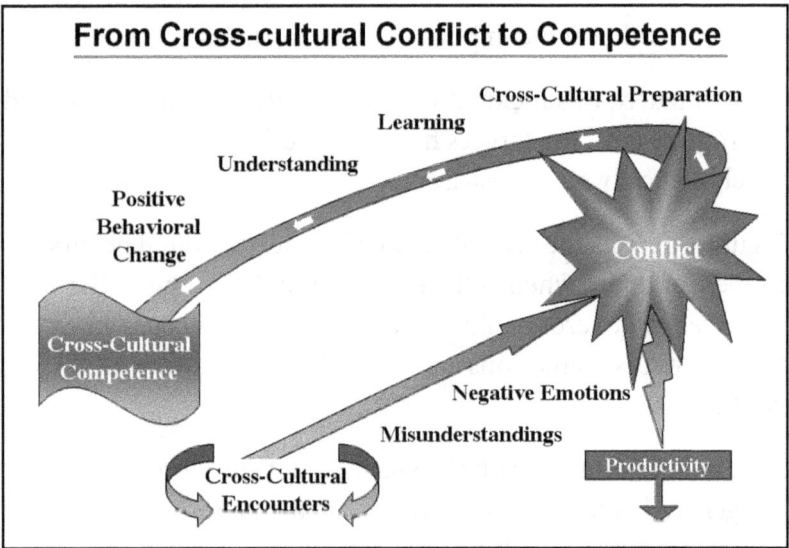

From Cross-cultural Conflict to Competence

Figure 9

The Unwanted Priests

I consulted for a Catholic Archdiocese that recruited foreign priests to fill positions in rural and urban churches. Many of these impatriates were from Africa, Latin America, and India—cultures generally much different than that of the United States.

Par for the course, neither the Americans nor the foreign recruits had cross-cultural preparation for working with each other. Because the cultural differences were pronounced and not understood, emotions ran high.

Although insulted and miserable, the foreign priests maintained their composure, but during my investigation, they related their feelings. They said the United States was not what they had expected. Coming from Africa, Latin America, and India, they thought living in the United States would be easy. They did not anticipate the loneliness, rejection, and indifference they experienced.

Here are a few of their comments from interviews:

- "He (senior American priest) said, 'You are here only insofar as we profit from you. If you are in trouble because you didn't know you had to pay taxes, I'm sorry, solve your own problem.'"

- "Even at mass sometimes, when we have the exchange of peace, people won't shake hands with us."

- "The loneliness can be terrible."

Adapting to U.S. culture is especially stressful for people from collective cultures where relationships and family are more highly valued than in individualistic cultures.

- "Every person here in America seems to be kind of isolated, individual. He is responsible for himself, and he has no community to fall back on."

- "Coming from a society where the family matters so much to a society where the individual matters most is very difficult."

Figure 10 depicts Individualism and Collectivism scores for just a few countries representative of the priests' cultures: Ethiopia, Costa Rica, Mexico, and India. You can see where Collectivism is on the left half, and Individualism is on the right, that the priests were from very Collectivistic, family- and relationship-oriented cultures. To be isolated in a foreign country was torturous for them.

Individualists, on the other hand, are perceived as more concerned about themselves and their immediate families than about building and maintaining relationships. And the United States has the highest Individualism score of all the nations researched. Compatibility between Collectivists and Individualists requires concerted effort.

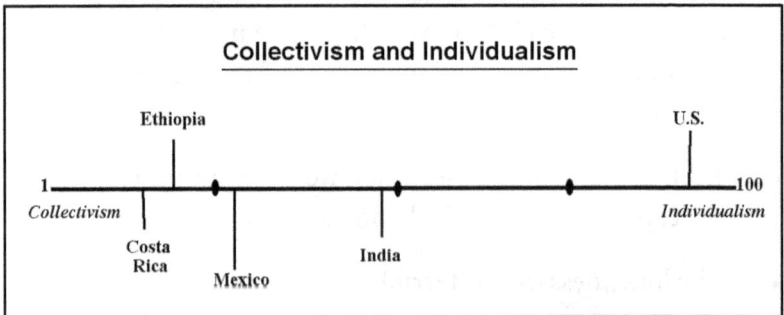

Collectivism and Individualism

Ethiopia   U.S.

1————————————————————100
Collectivism   Individualism

Costa Rica   India

Mexico

Figure 10

The case of The Unwanted Priests can also be described as workplace bullying. It has many of the earmarks:

- It took place over a long period of time.

- The behaviors occurred repeatedly.

- The targets were perceived as different, and also as better than the bullies, because all the foreign priests had graduate degrees, which the American priests did not.

- The goal was to undermine them and drive them away.

Although the targets hung in there, they suffered psychologically. One of the interviewees reported an American priest had commented, "What are you doing here, anyway? You have a Ph.D. Why don't you go home and use it?"

Cross-cultural preparation before expecting the American priests and foreign recruits to work together would have prevented most of the anxiety and culture-based conflict from developing. Their environment could have been conducive to high performance and productivity, rather than to creating a cauldron of emotions. Clearly, the head-in-the-sand mentality is far more expensive than being prepared upfront.

When people are aware of the other side's cultural expectations and respect the consequences of violating those expectations, they can learn to manage their knee-jerk reactions.

By the way, the term corporation can easily be substituted for archdiocese. Problems and results are the same.

"It's harder and harder for kids to change once the pattern is set and time goes on."

~ Leonard Eron, Psychologist,
University of Illinois
at Chicago

CHAPTER

Bad Apples Cost a Bushel: One Can Spoil the Whole Basket

When morale is low, as it is around Bad Apples, employees find many excuses for skipping work on a whim: it's too hot, it's too cold, it's raining or snowing too hard, "I'm too stressed," or "I deserve it, the company owes me."

Unscheduled absenteeism is so pervasive that companies have to budget for it. On average, they set aside more than six percent of the total budget—that means if you have a $500,000 budget, its value is reduced by $30,000—money you could use for something better than paying for unproductive time. If you have a $100 million budget, the value goes down by $6 million. What a waste!

Now consider that only one-third of unscheduled absenteeism is due to personal illness. Much of the other two-thirds is due to low morale associated with workplace conflict (Fig. 11). The cost of lost work time due to just bullying is $76 billion per year in the United States. Absenteeism increases to the tune of $14 billion per year nationwide. Performance declines, productivity drops, employee turnover increases, and the numbers of formal complaints and lawsuits rise. Of course, when these cases are publicized, the organization's reputation is tarnished, as it becomes recognized as a hostile workplace.

The Impact of Employee Conflict

Employee Conflict

Reputation — Lost Work Time

Lawsuits — *Organizational Impact* — Absenteeism

Employee Turnover — Performance

Productivity

Figure 11

As a company owner or a manager, what would you do if you suddenly learned several of your best employees were thinking of leaving? You would probably start scrambling to provide incentives so these hard working employees would stay with you, or you would have to start recruiting. Replacing employees is not only a pain in your neck, but also, it's very expensive in many ways.

If your company is retaining a bully, you may as well start recruiting, because your employees are actively looking for new jobs.

For whatever reason, if your company is retaining a bully, you may as well start recruiting, because your employees are actively looking for new jobs—both the targets and the employees who witness the bullying over long periods of time. And the bullying is costing the company a bundle of dollars.

Consider these statistics from the 2007 U.S. Workplace Bullying Survey:

- Sixty-four percent of targets are driven out of their jobs by the bully: 40 percent quit, 24 percent are fired.

- The loss of only 40 percent of targets, those who quit, accounts for the loss of 21 million employees. Another 12 percent, the witnesses of bullying, also leave.

More from Dr. Gary Namie of Work Doctor, Inc.:

- Annual replacement costs of managers and employees due to bullying averages more than $16 million in an average Fortune 500 company.

- Only a 2% drop in productivity due to bullying costs more than $8 million annually in an average Fortune 500 company.

- In the U.K. (and probably more so in the U.S.), bullying costs businesses 80 million lost workdays annually.

Gallup Management Journal:

- Twenty-four percent of U.S. employees, overall, would fire their boss if they could. These are unengaged, unhappy employees. Of the *actively* disengaged employees, 51 percent would fire their boss.

- Employees who would like to fire their boss won't recommend their company for employment or its products and services.

Recent research shows employee attitudes relate to business-unit outcomes: employee turnover, customer satisfaction and loyalty, safety, productivity, and profitability criteria. Bullied employees are likely to have negative attitudes—driving down business-unit outcomes.

Common sense dictates bullies' behaviors cost organizations great sums of money in terms of damage to targets, witnesses, and employers. The costs are both tangible and intangible (Fig. 12).

Tangible Costs
- Turnover: recruitment, interviewing, hiring, training, loss of talent/expertice
- Absenteeism/Lost productivity
- Workers' compensation
- Disability insurance: Short- and long-term
- Legal action against organization
- Consultant's fees for bully rehabilitation

Intangible Costs
- Employee sabotage: delaying projects/withholding materials and information
- Low morale: customer service/dissatisfaction, lack of employee engagement, loss of preferred vendors
- Difficult recruitment and retention
- Tarnished reputation: unfriendly workplace, low opinion of products/services
- Bully retention continues the destructive and costly cycle

Figure 12

When employers choose to retain bullies, mistakenly thinking their value to the organization by far offsets their cost, they fail to consider the intangible expenses at even the most obvious level—once again assuming the ostrich stance and burying their heads in the sand.

"We're [corporations] beyond lean and mean. We're anorexic and vicious."

~ Corliss Olson, Labor Educator, University of Wisconsin Extension's School for Workers

CHAPTER 10

The Bottom Line Thrives on Polished-Apple Behavior

O h, how smoothly things run in our homes when the kids are at peace with one another, busy, and mentally engaged in productive activities! It's the same in organizations when employees are at peace with one another and engaged in their work.

Peaceful productivity contributes to the two basic ways of increasing the bottom line: cut costs and/or sell more. For example:

- When insurance agents improved their Emotional Intelligence (EI) competence, their sales jumped 15 to 21 percent, recovering the training investment in just one month.

- In a 1996 study of a global food and beverage company, David McClelland, Social Psychologist and achievement motivation expert, found that when senior managers had a critical mass of EI capabilities, their divisions outperformed yearly earnings goals by 20 percent. Division leaders without that critical mass underperformed by almost the same amount.

- Good relationships improve working environment and reduce employee turnover. Every employee who leaves an organization costs it at least an additional year's salary. Consider the costs of the exit interview, recruitment, interview time, training, decreased productivity during the learning period, decreased efficiency of everyone who works with a new hire, etc.

- At L'Oreal, the cosmetics company, sales agents who were selected for their strengths in these competencies had 63 percent less turnover during their first year.

- At a national life insurance company, those sales agents who were weak in self-awareness, self-management, and management of relationships sold policies with an average face value of $54,000, but those who were strong in those areas sold policies averaging $114,000.

Molson Coors, a beverage company, found its engaged employees were five times less likely to have safety incidents. The average yearly cost for safety incidents of an engaged employee was only $63, compared to $392 for an unengaged employee.

So Molson Coors went to work strengthening employee engagement and …

- *Saved* $2 million in one year, solely due to the decrease in safety incidents

- *Saved* more than $2 million in performance-related costs by increasing the engagement level of their sales teams.

In another example, Caterpillar, the maker of heavy construction and mining equipment ...

- Saved $9 million in one year from decreased attrition, absenteeism, and overtime in a European plant

- *Increased* output by 70 percent in less than four months in an Asian-Pacific plant

- *Increased* profit by $2 million

- *Increased* customer satisfaction by 34 percent at a start-up plant.

What did these companies do to improve employee engagement and performance? Overall, they improved communication (another soft skill that pays large dividends). They took the following steps to learn more about what their employees wanted and what they needed to do their jobs, and, in turn, to clarify what was expected from the employees:

A. **Measured Engagement** by asking employees the *Gallup Management Journal's* 12-Questions (GMJ 12Q) on How Do You Feel About Your Work?

1. Do you know what is expected of you at work?

2. Do you have what you need to do your work right?

3. At work, do you have opportunity everyday to do what you do best?

4. Have you received recognition/praise for doing good work in the last seven days?

5. Does your supervisor, or someone at work, seem to care about you?

6. Is there someone at work who encourages your development?

7. Do your opinions seem to count at work?

8. Does the mission of your company make you feel your job is important?

9. Are your fellow employees committed to doing quality work?

10. Do you have a best friend at work?

11. In the last 6 months, has someone at work talked about your progress?

12. In the last year, have you had opportunities at work to learn and grow?

B. **Identified Barriers** to engagement: Did employees have the information and materials they needed as well as a favorable working environment?

C. **Developed Communication Strategies.** They started showing more appreciation and understanding to employees. They made sure employees knew how they could contribute, and listened carefully to what employees were saying.

D. **Evaluated Human Resource Practices,** including how HR handled negative employee behaviors.

E. **Held Managers Accountable** for demonstrating organizational values, for the development of team members, and for results.

What does this mean to you and your organization?

- Bullies are not engaged employees, so focusing on improving employee engagement tends to expose them.

- It's encouraging and a great example for other corporations that these behemoth employers—Molson Coors and Caterpillar—were able to change their behaviors toward their employees. And, in response, the employees improved *their* behaviors as they began to feel appreciated.

Happy, engaged employees perform a whopping 20 percent better! They are 87 percent less likely to leave the organization. Why the improvement? They have better relationships with their managers and feel valued by their employers. Best of all, they aren't being kicked around by bullies while managers and employers bury their heads in the sand.

Happy, engaged employees perform a whopping 20% better! They are 87% less likely to leave the organization.

Take action. Plan what you're going to do to help yourself. Where you start depends on where you are in terms of defining bullying, the size and location of your organization, company policies, number and status of your allies, and other factors.

The important thing is to make an action plan and get started. It may change often, but you will be acting assertively and be in greater control, rather than acting passively and being a victim. Keep in mind the words of Ralph Waldo Emerson, "What lies behind us and what lies before us are tiny matters compared to what lies within us."

Selected References

Bardwick, Judith M. 2008. *One Foot Out the Door*. NY: AMACOM.

Buss, A.H., and M.P. Perry. 1992. *The aggression questionnaire*. Journal of Personality and Social Psychology 63, 452-450.

CCH 2005. *Costly problem of unscheduled absenteeism continues to perplex employers*. Riverwoods, IL, www.hr.cch.com.

Clark, Josh. 1997. *The business of bullying: Nasty bosses and co-workers cause turnovers and absenteeism in America's workplaces*. April 6. The Sunday Paper, www.sundaypaper.com

Cowie, Helen 1999. *Adult bullying*. Report of a Working Party, University of Surrey, Roehampton.

De Becker, Gavin. 1997. *The Gift of Fear*. New York: Dell Publishing.

Goleman, Daniel. 2004. *What makes a leader?* Harvard Business Review Nov/Dec.

Goleman, Daniel. 1998. *Working with Emotional Intelligence*. NY: Bantam Books.

Gurchiek, Kathy. *Fudge! Sugar! Watch your #*?/@%! Language*. SHRM Online. www.shrm.org/hrnews-published/articles/CMS-025516.asp.

Hofstede, Geert. 1984. *Culture's Consequences*. Newbury Park, CA: Sage.

Harter, James K., Frank L. Schmidt, and Theodore L. Hayes. 2002. *Business-unit-level relationship between employee satisfaction. Employee engagement, and business outcomes: A meta-analysis*. Journal of Applied Psychology 87, No. 2: 268-279.

Lockwood, Nancy R. 2007. *Leveraging employee engagement for competitive advantage: HR's strategic role*. SHRM: Research Quarterly, March.

Lutgen-Sandvik, Pamela, Sarah J Tracy, and Jess K. Alberts. 2006. *Burned by bullying in the American workplace: Prevalence, perception, degree, and impact*. Journal of Management Studies.

McFarland, Jean R. **www.BadAppleSolutions.com**

McFarland, Jean R. **www.BulliesAmongUs.blogspot.com**

McFarland, Jean R. **www.FifthDimensionStrategies.com**

McFarlin, Susan K., William Fals-Stewart, Debra A. Major and Elaine M. Justice. 2001. *Alcohol use and workplace aggression: An examination of perpetration and victimization.* Journal of Substance Abuse 13 no. 3:303-321.

Namie, Gary. 2006. *Bullies are too expensive to keep.* WorkDoctor.com/defined.html.

Namie, Gary, and Ruth Namie. 2003. *The Bully at Work.* Naperville, IL: Sourcebooks.

Newby, Jonica. May 5, 2005. *Corporate psychopaths.* www.abc.net.au/catalyst/stories/s1360571.htm (accessed December 12, 2007).

Ott, Bryant, and Emily Killham. 2007. *Would you fire your boss?* Gallup Management Journal, September 13. www.gmj.gallup.com.

Parry, Hazel. 2007. *Six ways to spot the workplace psychopath lurking in your office.* dpa German Press Agency. March 21. www.rawstory.com/news/dpa/Six_ways_to_spot_the_workplace_psyc_03212007.html.

Pech, Richard, and Bret Slade, 2006. *Employee disengagement: Is there evidence of a growing problem?* Handbook of Business Strategy 7 No. 1: 21-25. Sheehan, Michael. 1999. *Workplace bullying: Responding with some emotional intelligence.* International Journal of Manpower 20. State University of New York at Buffalo, Research Institute on Addictions. Buffalo, NY, 14203-1016, USASUNDAY.

Sutton, Robert I. 2007. *The No Asshole Rule.* NY: Warner Business Books.

Tracy, Sarah J., Jess K. Alberts, and Kendra Dyanne Rivera. 2007. *How to bust the office bully. Eight tactics for explaining workplace abuse to decision-makers.* ASU, The Hugh Downs School of Human Communication Report #0701.

Workplace Bullying Institute and Zogby International. 2007. *U.S. Workplace Bullying Survey.* www.workkplacebulyinginstitute.org.

Yamada, David C. and Gary Namie. *The 'Healthy Workplace' Bill A model act to provide legal redress for targets of workplace bullying, abuse, and harassment without regard to protected class status.* Suffolk University Law School and The Workplace Bullying & Trauma Institute. www.onthejobsolutions.com/bully/healthyworkbill.pdf (accessed July 3, 2008).

Zimbardo, Philip. 2007. *The Lucifer Effect: Understanding How Good People Turn Evil.* NY: Random House Trade Paperbacks.

Anti-Bullying Websites

Foundations and Institutes

- The Work Doctor   www.workdoctor.com
- Workplace Bullying Institute   www.bullyinginstitute.org
- Dignity at Work Now   www.dignityatworknow.org.uk
- Workplace Bullying   www.workplacebullying.co.uk
- The New Workplace Institute   www.newworkplaceinstitute.org

Blogs

- Dr. Jean R. McFarland
  www.bulliesamongus.blogspot.com

- Dr. Uma Gupta's Official Story
  www.umaguptatheofficialstory.typepad.com/officialstory/tipoff.html

Neither the author nor publisher takes any responsibility for the continuation or ongoing quality of these sites or the damage or results that might occur as a result of viewing or of using suggestions on these sites.

If you know the enemy
and know yourself,
you need not fear the result
of a hundred battles.
If you know neither the enemy
nor yourself,
you will succumb in every battle.

~ Sun Tzu

Fifth Dimension Strategies
Resources and Services

Dr. Jean McFarland is President of Fifth Dimension Strategies, a consulting firm focused on improving the quality and productivity of the work environment through the understanding of cultural differences and the elimination of the negative impact of bullying behaviors. McFarland often works with a network of business associates, including Mark Lewis, Ph.D., of Business Partners Network and Bonnie Mattick, MAEd., MBA, of Mattick & Associates.

Professional Speaking

Jean McFarland speaks on cross-cultural competence in business and workspace culture and behaviors for conventions and organizations. Dr. McFarland can be contacted at info@fifthDimensionStrategies.com.

Cross-Cultural Focus: Workshops and Consulting Services

Workshops and consulting services are available from Fifth Dimension Strategies and are detailed at www.fifthdimensionstrategies.com/workshops.html

Aligning Management Practices with Cultural Expectations
One-Day Workshop
Participants of this workshop leave with knowledge and tools needed to predict and understand culture-based workplace behaviors. They identify their own managerial styles and those of global employees, then practice using their knowledge and tools to adapt their communication and management styles to fit those expected by their employees.

Managing Global Employees (MGE) Workshop
Two-Day Workshop

In this workshop, participants examine what makes effective managers as well as not-so-effective managers. To do this, we help you identify and describe personal management practices. We provide tools to foresee and surmount constraints to managing global employees. To further customize the workshop, we address your specific countries and cultures of concern.

Advanced MGE Workshop

Participants use the knowledge, tools, and skills acquired from the MGE Workshop to focus in-depth on a specific culture. Recommended for leaders and managers who work with global employees primarily from one culture and for potential expatriates.

Managing U.S. Employees (MUSE)

Global managers of U.S. employees participate in learning that is focused on U.S. culture and enhanced with follow-up coaching.

Multicultural Team Building

Team members learn to understand and predict culture-based behaviors that impact team performance and to leverage them to team advantage. Team members should participate in MGE-equivalent learning and follow with team coaching.

Cross-Cultural Negotiation for Global Managers

U.S. leaders and managers should have MGE-equivalent knowledge. They learn cross-cultural negotiating strategies that they can apply to target cultures.

Multicultural Team Building for Cross-Cultural Negotiations
Team members learn to understand and predict culture-based behaviors that impact team performance as they acquire expertise in team self-management. They learn to bridge cultural gaps and to strategize cross-cultural negotiation processes for use with target cultures.

Workspace Culture and Behaviors: Workshops and Consulting Services

Employee Conflict – *The Destructive Power of One Bad Apple.*

Bullies at Work – *Strategies for Dealing with Costs and Behaviors.*

Employee Engagement – *Turning the Tide on Performance.* McFarland, J.R. & Mattick, B.F.

Articles (at www.fifthdimensionstrategies.com/articles.html)

Cross-Culture Business Savvy Articles

- Catch the Culture to Market Internationally

- Understanding Gestures is the Tip of the Iceberg

- Preparing to Predict and Interpret Cultural Behaviors

- Are you a Savvy Cross-Cultural Manager?

- Cultural Differences - the leading cause of Merger Failures

Conflict & Culture Articles

- Cross-cultural Conflict at Work

- Are You a Cross-culturally Savvy Manager?

Expatriate Articles

- International Employees Plead for Education and Assistance in Adjusting to Living in Foreign Cultures

- Cultural Incompetence: Do You Know What Your Employees Are Doing?

Newsletter

A periodic newsletter is available on line at www.fifthdimensionstrategies.com/news.html

INDEX

A

Absenteeism 26, 39, 41, 49, 52, 57, 61
Aggression 3, 4, 6, 27, 61, 62
Anger 21, 30, 44
Anger Management 30
Antidotes 22, 25

B

Bad Apple v, 2, 3, 6, 9, 10, 14, 15, 21, 22, 23, 25, 29, 30, 33, 37, 40, 41, 49, 69
Behavior, Aggressive 4
Behavior, Culture-based 37, 42, 43, 68, 69
Bully
    Academic 8, 12
    Bosses 7, 17, 18, 39, 51, 52, 61, 62
    Conservationist 18
    Corporate 13, 37
    Doctor 1
    Priests 44, 45, 46, 47
    Small Business 25
Buss and Perry 3, 6, 61

C

Caterpillar 57, 59
Collectivism 45, 46
Communication 2, 30, 36, 40, 43, 57, 58, 67, 74
Competence 4, 31, 43, 44, 67, 71
Conflict 9, 35, 43, 47, 49, 69
Costs of Bullying v, 26, 27, 34, 37, 39, 41, 49, 51, 52, 56, 61, 69, 74
Critic, Critical 12
Cross-cultural Competence/Incompetence 40, 43, 44, 67, 74
Cultured-based Behavior 37, 42, 43, 68, 68
Cuss Control Academy 30

O

Olson, Corliss 54

P

Paranoia 32
Perform, Performance 4, 8, 18, 35, 38, 39, 40, 41, 47, 50, 55, 56, 57, 59, 68, 69, 71
Presenteeism 39
Productivity 21, 34, 35, 39, 43, 47, 50, 51, 52, 55, 56, 67, 76

S

Screamer 11, 25
Sun Tzu 64

T

Two-faced Scoundrel 11, 14, 15

W

Workplace Aggression Behaviors 4
Workplace Bullying Survey 51, 62

Y

Yamada, David 24, 63

About the Author

This book has developed from Jean McFarland's integration of her professional work and her personal experiences as a target of bullying managers and co-workers. She provides a practical guide to reporting and handling bullying, improving communications and raising morale by helping people speak up and speak out.

Dr. McFarland is a consultant, professional speaker, and educator, specializing in performance improvement in corporations and organizations. She focuses on the benefits of reducing the human and corporate cost of bullying behaviors in the workplace, and developing competence to communicate with and to manage people from diverse cultures.

As president of Fifth Dimension Strategies, McFarland has worked with people of Fortune 500 companies, universities, and other organizations. She presents speeches, workshops, and seminars on improving cross-cultural competence and management, re-engaging employees, and dealing with bullying behaviors, to improve relations and cut costs in the global workforce.

McFarland resides in Scottsdale, Arizona, and may be reached at info@FifthDimensionStrategies.com or www.FifthDimensionStrategies.com.

* 9 7 8 0 9 8 2 0 5 0 8 0 4 *